Mo
Speaks

Monique Robinson

Copyrights

Mo Speaks Notes

Dedication

The day you left; all I could do was cry.
Deep down inside, no one knew you were
going to die.
When they told me you were dead, it felt like a
lie.
All I could say was that's not my sister you're
telling a lie.
My heart stopped, and I dropped.
You left me with no goodbye.
My little sister is dead.
I'm left behind to cry.
On the day you left, it felt like I had died.
I saw mom fall to her knees and cry.
I never thought I would see someone die.
Nowadays, all I do is cry.
I look up to the sky and say goodbye.

PS: Thank you for being my sister, partner in
crime, and best friend. I love you and continue
to Rest In Peace!

R.I.P Darielle Robinson
02/16/1996-01/30/2002

Inspirational Corner

The Pressing

The pain is necessary.
The loud scream and what seems like the end.
The pressing is so hard to comprehend.
You're fighting against what you don't understand.
God is shaping you to pull out what's within.
The stretching you're feeling is something you
can't shake.
The world around you is moving like an
earthquake.
This season of isolation you can't take.
If you push through this pressing, something will
break.
Trust the process and be quick on the uptake.
When you make it through this, you'll turn out to
be great.
In order to get what's good, the pressing comes
with weight.
Try your best to keep from stressing.
In order to get to the blessing, you have to go
through some pressing.

Champion in Me

There is a champion in me.
One whom I now see.
I've been broken, misused, and abused.
I pushed on.
There was heartache, mistakes, and bad breaks.
I had to own.
Still, that champion in me fought to stay strong.
I was ridiculed and perplexed.
I didn't allow the opinions of others to have me
vexed.
My truth to them was taken out of context.
I fought the good fight with all my might.
I didn't know what was coming next.
I pushed through the crowd of doubters.
The clock ticked with the passing hours.
I stood firm with nothing left to see.
I knew there was a champion in me.
Even when I felt like my hope was gone.
The champion in me was like a lion it roared on!

When the Fight Is Gone

When your fight is gone; you have to keep holding
on.
The race is not given to the swift, nor the strong.
It's given to the one who can endure until the end.
It's not always easy in this life of sin.
You have to push through the hard times.
Only you know where your story begins.
The courage you need is deep within.
You're waging war against yourself.
Value your life and place your pride on the shelf.
In this life, you can't trust luck.
By giving up, you'll self-destruct.
Remember to never be someone's pawn.
No matter what it looks like.
Keep hanging on, even when the fight is gone.

No Pain No Gain

You can't move through life not going through
anything.
Not one experience should be taken lightly or in
vain.
When traveling this road, it's hard not to complain.
Choosing the narrow route sometimes it's hard to
sustain.
Wise words, no pain, no gain.
The wrong that was done set in like a stain.
Trying to stay afloat when it's tough to maintain.
The knowledge that is given can be too much to
contain.
You rally everyone together like it's time to
campaign.
Still, I say no pain no gain.
Your actions are so plain and mundane.
You get tired of pushing forward.
You're so drained.
With the light up ahead, your strength you regain.
The plans for your life you attempt to ascertain.
The events in your life are linked together like a
chain.
When someone tries to help you tell them to stay
in their lane.

The lives we were given are not all the same.
Some of us stand tall while others fall like the rain.
The point that was made will remain.
Life is not easy but no pain, no gain.

Counted Out

You're not like everyone else.
People can't seem to understand.
When God created you, he had a special plan.
To the world, you were lost and confused.
The problem was they ignored the power of God in
you.
They counted you out without a doubt.
Never thinking twice just following the clout.
You're strange to them and stood out.
They had the directions and still went off route.
What people fail to understand.
Is the same ability wasn't given to every man.
You fought through the rough seas to get to dry
land.
Navigating through and following God's plan.
In every circle, there's a scout whose true
intentions are doubted.
There are lies in their mouth like a bass or a trout.
If you have to scream, stand firm, and shout.
I was always the one, but you counted me out.

There's a Purpose for The Pain

You're broken down.
You can't explain.
The thoughts in your head have you going insane.
There are no words to make it plain.
I want you to know there's a purpose for the pain.
You're acting out and hard to restrain.
Your life was thrown into a hurricane.
Everyone is saying be happy as if it's a joke.
They say to enjoy this life you should be stoked.
With this whirlwind called life, who do you
blame?
You're moving through your day-to-day feeling
ashamed.
I want you to know there's a purpose for the pain.
The stress in your life is on your brain.
Everyone will be there.
That's what they proclaim.
The pain has you feeling strange.
All you could say is it's time for a change.
You can stand your ground no need to be
deranged.
Shout to the heavens when you're not feeling the
same.
I've said all that.
It still isn't masking this thing.

I want to remember there's a purpose for the pain.

14

Trust Him

Remember to keep God first.
The devil hunger and thirsts.
We're all in this together.
This isn't coerced.
Treat a blessing like a blessing, a curse like a
curse.
Trust the path you're on even when you've done
wrong.
If your hope is gone, you have to fight to stay
strong.
Instead of stressing, you have to keep on pressing.
There's no need for guessing.
Life is full of lessons.
You can forget what they say.
There's no need to impress them.
Take a step back and show God that you trust him.
Do what you can.
Trust God's plan.
If you don't understand, know that God can.
Keep your head to the sky.
Trust the power you'll win.

Untitled

The storms bring the rain.
Life's hurt brings you pain.
When facing trials and tribulations, you'll never be
the same.
When you're at your lowest, no one remembers
your name.
You learn that life is a precious gift, not a game.
Remember each stage of your life is a phase.
Don't get caught up in the maze.
Today is today.
Tomorrow is tomorrow.
Bear this life.
Don't carry that sorrow.

Let Them Go

When everyone turns their back on you; let them
go.
When they only want the yes, and refuse the no.
Let them go.
When they take more than they give.
They don't care how you live.
Let them go.
When they're like crabs in a bucket and want you
to move like their puppet.
Let them go.
When they add more stress and leave you feeling
depressed.
Let them go.
When they bring pain and shame, *let them go.*
When they refuse to change, and they're stuck on
staying the same.
Let them go.
When their presence causes your peace to cease.
Let them go.
If they're not helping you grow, *let them go.*

Pray

When you can't seem to find your way, PRAY
When you've been broken down by life and can't
find the words to say. PRAY
When the world stands against you, and the ones
you love have gone astray. PRAY
When the pain seems as if it won't end, and you
can't pull the power from within. PRAY
When you've given it your best, and still can't pass
the test. PRAY
When you've put more out than you've gotten
back in. PRAY
When you can't stand you kneel, PRAY.
All who have led astray will soon find their way
when they PRAY.

Seesaw

It's the ups and downs.
The back and forth.
The smiles and frowns.
The life we're living is an everyday choice.
We're out here living aimlessly with no remorse.
It's the push-off and the breakdown.
Your feet are firmly planted on the ground.
The feeling of being high up and the sudden fall
back down.
You find that one person that helps you balance it
out.
You go high.
What goes up must come down.
Gravity pulls you back down to earth.
The repeated cycle causes too much hurt.
You're learning the balance with no expert.
You must figure out how to work through the
flaws.
This life moves just like a seesaw.

If You Knew My Story

If you knew my story, you wouldn't be so quick to
judge.
You wouldn't give useless opinions and tell silly
lies.
You walk around like you're holding a grudge.
Truth be told.
You don't know the time it took to break this
mold.
Let the light shine on me as I gleam like gold.
It's my duty to tell the world the stories untold.
You weren't there for the sleepless nights.
When I sat up praying to God, thinking fight, or
flight.
I overcame the obstacles that were placed in front
of me at birth.
Where were you when the doctor told my mom to
choose between me or her?
People like you judge without knowing all the
facts.
I jumped the hurdles of life.
I fought back tears like I was orchestrating an act.
You all sat back, saying I'll never be this or that.
If you knew my story, you wouldn't open your
mouth, nor utter the slightest negative word.

I hit my knees and pray.
It wasn't a man, but it was God's voice I heard.
Everyone's so quick to tell my story better than I
am.
Without knowing what they don't see.
You don't know how hard I worked when it hurt.
I beat the odds.
It's difficult for them to understand.
This anointing on my life, only the strong survive.
It's for God to get the glory.
When it's all said and done.
I promise you won't have to worry.
I'll keep it simple for you without being in a hurry.
If I had something negative to say, you'd grab a
chair, and sit down in a scurry.
I speak my truth even unto you.
Things would be different if you knew my story.

Making Peace with Me

I close my eyes.
I begin to meditate.
The thoughts in my head, I can't seem to
manipulate.
The old me is dying.
I'm fighting.
I have to concentrate.
I know it's time to elevate.
I'm making the moves.
I'm taking a chance.
You get stuck in a routine like you're caught in a
trance.
The world around me is moving in fear.
They're afraid of the unknown facts of what's
near.
Despite being surrounded, I pressed ahead to
remain grounded.
This life is like a war zone.
People wander around looking for a home.
I'm finding my peace while they're all in cahoots.
They can't center themselves.
They won't dig deep.
You can't find something you never looked for.
Every opportunity given is not a real open door.

I'm learning to discern right from wrong.
Sometimes to get it right.
You have to walk this path alone.

Light at the End of the Tunnel

Did you let that storm break you down?
You need to get up and fight back.
Show the devil he's a clown.
Today has been one of those days.
You felt like you couldn't win.
You sit back engaging in foolishness.
The devil is at it again.
You see me.
I can speak on it.
I once was you.
I lost faith and I'm not pleading my case.
I had no real clue.
Times got hard.
Instead of trusting in God, I thought it was for me
to do.
I didn't know if I kept walking by faith.
I'd get through.
If you have to cry, then cry.
Don't give up.
You must try.
This road of life isn't easy.
It's tough like a jungle.
While pouring into others, it can be messy so grab
a funnel.

You're not alone in this.
Don't lose your sight, and don't be disgruntled.
Look up!
There's light at the end of the tunnel.

Misguided

The route I was given left me off track.
There are too many times in life I had to double
back.
I have one guide saying go left.
The other says go right.
I'm stuck between a rock and a hard place.
The space is tight.
I'm searching for what I hope is the right GPS.
Trying to find the right direction puts me under
stress.
How can you trust the path you're on?
I don't know if it's the way.
I'm learning from others to trust the path and not
delay.
When we fall hard, we tend to stray.
Walk with a stride even when your faith and doubt
collide.
Don't fall for others' pride.
Push back doesn't subside.

Step Out

You weren't born to fit in.
You aren't who you were then.
Don't hold yourself back or stop your stride.
Let go of that ego and drop your pride.
Take time to see you're the one who matters.
When you walk into a new room, ignore the
chatter.
Your light shines differently.
It'll never go dim.
You find your true way when you learn to trust
him.
With every opportunity, you make it count.
Don't follow the crowd for the clout.
Don't hold yourself back and live in doubt.
Go against the grain be you and step out.

Sleeping On Me

I complain about what others don't see when they
look at me.
I'm the one who's stopping me.
I never focused on my good qualities.
Instead, I choose the bad ones to see.
With all the gifts I've been blessed with, I don't
understand why it's hard for me.
I overlook the great.
I slept on me.
My mind manipulated me.
I've overcome the worst of messes.
I turned a blind eye to what was best.
I got angry and ready to flee.
I looked around.
It was as if everyone was sleeping on me.
If I'm not being a critic of myself, I'm choosing
the wrong route.
It's bad for my health.
I can't get mad at what they don't see.
When all along, I'm the one sleeping on me.

Patient in Prayer

The hardest thing for us to do is wait.
We rush through life like a horse breaking out the
gate.
Be still and trust the silence.
If you're unsure, ask God for his guidance.
Don't let one failed mission cause you to lack
confidence.
Go to God in prayer that's the true entrance.
You don't always get what you want, so don't try
to take it.
You must know that God has it all.
Trust him and be patient.
Don't believe the devil's lies.
He spreads them like cancer.
Be patient in prayer that's the real answer.

Until I Knew My Worth

There are constant letdowns.
Then, random outbursts when battling depression.
I was making excuses for the mishandling and
neglect.
I allowed an unhealed person to tear me down and
self-project.
I accepted the lie.
That I was dumb and naïve.
I believe that's all I'd ever be.
I never fought back.
I knew there was more.
I knew I couldn't take it.
The soldier inside me prepared for war.
That's when I came to the realization.
That I couldn't handle this without an altercation.
I was no longer taking the beatings of life.
I laced up my boots.
I prepared myself to move without strife.
I kicked down the door to hatred.
No longer would I take it.
If I kept allowing negativity, I knew I wouldn't
make it.
Honestly, it was time for a rebirth.

I couldn't understand why things came up against
me.
Things came upon me like it was all coerced.
I chose myself over them.
I looked myself in the eyes and got it together like
a hem.
I knew the truth about myself.
It had to be unearthed.
I never understood why I fought so hard.
That was until I knew my worth.

The Calm Before the Storm

The stillness is quiet in the night.
You feel it in your gut.
It's coming, but it's out of sight.
You've worked hard for this blessing.
You take your time in this peaceful period to worry
less and stop stressing.
You've dealt with difficult matters.
They hit you left and right like a title wave.
You've had to stand strong when you barely knew
how to behave.
The time is now and there's no more time to waste.
Get in line and take your place.
The storm that is coming wasn't sent to break you.
Anything God allows was sent to make you.
Hit your knees and pray.
Don't wait.
There isn't room for delay.
This is why you were born.
Remember in life things get hard.
There's always the calm before the storm.

Valley Experience

The Weight of the World

The weight of the world is on my chest.
It's like stress that I wear as a vest.
With so much mess around me, I need some rest.
The pressure of life has left me with no peace.
With all the nonsense, I wish it would cease.
The walls are closing in from all the pain within.
The weight of the world has to be sin.
This weight has me losing sleep.
An understanding that runs deep.
The weight of the world knocks me off of my feet.
With no words to describe the feeling of defeat.
It's like painting with no brush.
The art is incomplete.
The weight of the world has me traumatized.
The weight of the world has me ignoring the truth
and believing the lies.
If you could look through my eyes, you'll see; that
maybe the weight of the world is me.

You Don't Know Me

Everyone thinks they know me because of what
they see.
How do you know what you see is me?
I laugh and joke in hope that no one will know.
The silent battles go on unnoticed.
I fight so hard to keep my focus.
A strong person is what you see.
But truth be told you don't know me.
I'm always looking out for others.
My family, friends, sisters, and brothers.
I speak my truth they say it's cap.
When they don't realize I'm trapped.
The stories untold are where it all begins.
If your glasses are broken, replace the lens.
I wrote it out with paper and pens.
I'm an open book is what they say.
They don't know I rip pages out every day.
I put it on a display for people to see.
The hardest thing is you don't know me.

Silent Battles

I'm running in circles trying to escape.
I'm no superhero so there's no need for a cape.
I can tell you this, or I can tell you that.
I constantly feel as if I'm under attack.
At the rate I'm going, there is no coming back.
I've dropped the ball, and my back is against the
wall.
With no one around me, who do I call?
I can't think straight.
I have too much on my plate.
The voices in my head have me feeling as if
someone's here.
The negative thoughts leave me with fear.
I'm trying to get away to grab my horse and
saddle.
Everyone has problems; they don't speak on those
silent battles.

Broken Pieces

Tears flowed down my face.
My heart is heavy and beating at a steady pace.
Everything that was together is now falling apart.
It's broken pieces from my shattered heart.
Broken pieces left all scattered.
There's glass slamming against the tile.
My heart has turned to ice like a cold case file.
With unanswered questions and a mystery so
sweet.
I lay down at night not seeming to find sleep.
All that's left is broken pieces for me to sweep.

Can You See That It's Me?

I stood the test of time to show you a love like
mine.
I never once questioned what was believed to be
divine.
I didn't run at the sign of trouble.
I stood tall and loved you double.
With what seems like explosives, not once judging
just seeking the motive.
While giving my heart as the votive.
I was always the one who stood out in the crowd.
I choose to wear a smile instead of a frown.
Even with no hope in sight, I chose to love you
with all my might.
Instead of giving up, I wanted to fight.
I asked myself could it be?
Why not pick up my bags and flee?
I trust my heart in your hands.
In times like this, we search for love on demand.
Without the lock, I had the key.
I want to know can you see that it's me.

Pain Is What I Feel

Pain is what I feel.
When you're not here, or when you are not near.
Pain is what I feel, and also what I fear.
Pain is what you put me through.
Pain is what I feel because of you.
Pain comes old, and pain comes new.
My pain is the fear of losing you.

When Will

When will you love me?
When will you tell me the truth?
When will you stop the lies?
When will you look me in the eyes?
When will you stop making me cry?
When will you try?
When will you stop saying what you can't do?
When will you realize I love you?
When will you accept me?
When will you make me happy?
When will you stop hurting me?
When will you see me as I saw you?

Looked Over

You were picked last when it was time to play.
Like the last little pup, you were left alone to get
up.
You were authentic yet looked over.
They passed you up as if you were a poser.
All the while, you're seeking answers and wanting
closure.
You stood at the top of the stairs for all to see.
No one noticed you; how could that be?
Like the sweetest fruit at the bottom of the basket.
They walked along as if you were in a casket.
In your rarest form, you were a four-leaf clover.
Most times the best people are the ones that are
looked over.

I'm Tired

I'm tired of your lies.
I'm tired.
I'm through.
I'm tired of the pain and sorrow I feel with you.
I'm tired of crying.
I'm tired of trying.
I'm tired of hearing what you said you're going to
do.
You know what?
I must be tired of you.

I Thought

I thought you me loved me.
I thought what we shared was there.
I thought that you would always be here.
I thought it would last.
I thought you had passed the test.
I guess what I thought wasn't the best.

Fighting the Me Within

I tell myself I can't.
I know deep down I can.
I'm running a race with no real plan.
I'm looking around for an enemy.
When my only enemy was me.
Like a child, I kick, fight, and scream.
I'm lost because I feel all of this is a scheme.
Whenever I think I'm doing great.
I'm filled with nothing but self-hate.
Could this be?
I'm battling me.
It's a struggle trying not to stress.
When the weight of life has me pressed.
I'm skating on ice that's thin.
The real truth is I'm fighting the me within.

Biggest Critic

To the world, I'm viewed as a hero.
When I look at myself, I see a zero.
People applaud me.
They tell me that I'm great.
I can't seem to see the value in myself for heaven's
sake.
I'm doing good.
I'm growing.
There are times that I beat myself up without even
knowing it.
The little ones look up to me.
It's me that they mimic.
They don't know I'm fighting myself.
I'm my own biggest critic.

What About Me

I broke bread with those who could care less about
me.
I was the shoulder that everyone cried on.
I fought hard for others when my hope was gone.
I pose one question: what about me?
I carried the weight and tried my best.
They still didn't see.
I'm always a phone call away.
Simply, a listening ear, and ready to pray.
I'm there for them even on my worst day.
What about me?
I tried to smile more than I cried.
All along deep inside, something had to die.
I checked on them.
I put my plans on pause.
The sad thing is that when I'm going through.
I can't even get a call.
I struggled to look for myself.
Whom I can't see.
I still pose the question: what about me?

Giving Too Much

I gave and I gave until I couldn't give anymore.
I pushed through even when my body was sore.
I fought so hard with all my might.
I'm fighting for something that is out of sight.
I'm giving in when I really want to step.
Imagine fighting for something when there's
nothing left.
I was told things like this would be hard; get ready
and prepare.
Every time I think about it, we play the hand we're
dealt.
They say life is not a game, but everyone is
playing.
Wait hear me out; no, really, I'm just saying.
This game is give or take.
It is not such?
I see clearly.
I noticed I was giving too much.

Trained by My Pain

The hidden truth made me this way.
I was given life lessons.
I was too young to pay.
The trauma from the pain I had to endure was
catastrophic.
I'm speaking up now on a sensitive topic.
I was taught to believe that this feeling was the
norm.
I never once questioned why it came in all forms.
I was left backstabbed, broken-hearted, and
betrayed.
My personal space was left to invade.
My hurt didn't matter.
I poured out my feelings like the liquid they
splatter.
It was hard enough moving through life not trying
to complain.
I never realized that I was trained by my pain.

Bleeding Out

I carried my feelings in a bag.
My heart was on my sleeve.
I held back as the trials in life were beating on me.
My feelings got hurt at times.
I wouldn't say a word.
I noticed that everyone had their fight and speaking
on mine was unheard.
Anything I would say was a problem.
When anyone came to me, I seem to be their
problem solver.
I would get so upset and clench my fist.
I'd cock back like a revolver.
I'm swinging at the air.
There's nothing to hit.
I try to voice my hurt.
I'm looked upon as a misfit.
I know I'm destined for greatness.
The life I'm living now isn't it.
I wanted them to see the hurt they caused.
I pushed past the doubt.
I was screaming on the inside.
No one noticed I was bleeding out.

Losing You Wasn't a Part of the Plan

I had it all figured out.
That's what I thought.
I was running reckless thinking I'd never get
caught.
It's funny.
I was caught by the very thing I thought I had so
much of.
Time ran out while I placed everything else above.
I took a moment that only came once for granted.
You told me to slow down and focus.
I complained and ranted.
With each moment that passed, I didn't see you
fading away.
You tried to prepare me for that coming day.
When it finally set in, I prayed.
I asked God for a delay.
I thought we had what seemed like forever.
If only I knew, I would lose you so soon.
Letting you go, I would never.
You gave me the knowledge I needed to get
through life.
That was clever.
I thought we'd make it through the rough patches
in life together.
When I lost you, I felt like I could barely stand.

Now, I have to push through this life alone.
Without your kind words and helping hand.
I never thought I'd be where I am.
Today, it's crazy.
I still don't understand.
When I mapped out my life, losing you wasn't part
of the plan.

Butterflies & Bliss

Something About You

Something about you makes me smile.
Something about you makes me frown.
It's something about you.
I don't know why.
There's something about you that makes me cry.
Something about you makes me love you through
the rain.
Something about you makes me love you through
the pain.
It's something about you that has me not knowing
what to say.
I ask myself what has me feeling this way?
Why does this something have me wanting to stay?
Maybe it's the love I have for you every day.

I Choose You

If I had a million choices, I'd still choose you.
Like the number one pick in the drafts, it's you I
have to have.
Whenever I'm low or feeling blue.
I find joy when I think of you.
With all the answers I still have no clue.
All I know is I choose you.
With a heart like yours, I couldn't resist.
This love with you, I'd be stupid to miss.
Your hugs are so soft, kisses so sweet.
Your radiant smile I couldn't dismiss.
I stand in a room surrounded by hearts, yet not
feeling the love.
When I'm around you, I want to fly like a dove.
It's as if we're the perfect fit like a glove.
If you were me, what would you do?
I'd hope you say, I still choose you.

Ray

A love like this, I can't describe.
I fell in love the moment I looked into your brown
eyes.
Many laughed and chuckled when I would
proclaim; *"that loving this man isn't the same."*
The way I would melt hearing your name.
Over the years, our love has grown with time.
This love we share is so divine.
People looked when I would say, *"one day he is
going be my bae."*
I remember the first time you had me crying in the
shower.
I fell apart like a broken tower.
I felt like I'd missed my hour.
The thought of you being in love with another
woman made me sour.
As time passed, we fought to see our love last.
Now, I sit back and laugh.
I told y'all one day; *"Ray would be my bae."*

When I First Saw You

When I first saw you, all I could do was smile.
The light of your glowing face, had me feeling like
I was out in space.
When I first saw you, I knew you were the one.
I thought to myself, *"he is that special someone."*
When I first saw you, I didn't know what to do.
When our eyes connected, I knew it was true.
The feeling caught me by surprise.
Somehow, I just knew you were the guy.

A Dream Come True

Being with you is like a dream come true.
I was smiling, blushing, and acting shy too.
I realize you're the boy from my dream.
Now, I smile because I'm with you.
You're the boy that made my dreams come true.
Laughter comes when I think of how I feel about
you.
I can finally say I'm happy.
I'm with someone that doesn't make me feel
crappy.
I had a dream that left me without a clue.
It wasn't until I met you.
I notice being with you is a dream come true.

My Life Without You

My life without you would be full of pain.
My life without you just wouldn't be the same.
My life without you I can't explain.
My life without you would leave my heart broken
in shame.
My life without you would leave me with no
words.
My life without you would crush my dreams.
My life without you would make me scream.
If I didn't have you in my life, I would be blue.
I can't see myself living life without you.

His Love

A love so pure it's hard to explain.
Many have told their version of the story.
It still sounds plain.
A feeling of peace when you're in his presence.
A feeling so unimaginable, it's difficult for it to
make sense.
He gives his love even when we don't deserve it.
He pours his heart out and still we curve it.
I'm talking about a love that trumps all others.
This love is deeper than what you get from your
sisters and brothers.
A life was given to prove this love.
Nothing else can be placed above.
One of the greatest things given was his love.

Choose Love

When everyone is being hateful.
You, be happy and grateful.
Choose to love no matter what the options may be.
People lack faith and don't believe what they can't
see.
When your heart is broken, and you're only given
betrayal as a token.
You still have to choose love.
When two hearts come together, nothing is placed
above.
I've found one thing clever.
The way love brings us together.
You can smile or cry.
Choose love and let it fly.

The Beauty in Your Eyes

The beauty in your eyes is the calm of a storm.
Although the waves are rough, you keep my heart
warm.
When I look into your eyes, I know that nothing
can bring me harm.
I have a clear vision.
I can see what you see.
I tell you.
It's the beauty in your eyes when you look at me.
Just like the stars that light up the night sky.
I promise I see the same twinkle in your eyes.
I'm captivated by your glance.
I'm mesmerized.
I feel so thrown off like a boat that capsized.
They say beauty is in the eye of the beholder.
I see they told no lies.
In all reality, I can't help but see.
The beauty in your eyes when you look at me.

My Mind

My mind is on you.
I don't know why.
My mind is like a cloud floating in the sky.
My mind is so gone.
I can't lie.
You're the reason that my mind is on a high.
My mind is like a leaf in the water as it flows.
Sometimes I feel like my mind comes and goes.
My mind is so focused on you.
My mind believes that our love is true.
My mind tells my heart that I love you.

I Carry You in My Heart

Even though we are far apart.
I still carry you in my heart.
You may not be near.
Still, the love we share is crystal clear.
Although life has brought about a change.
The space you hold in my heart can't be
rearranged.
If I can't walk to get to you, I'll waddle.
For our love, I'll go full throttle.
Whether we're close together, or 1,000 miles apart.
Remember, I'll always carry you in my heart.

Butterflies

Like the eagle flying high in the sky, you give me
butterflies.
I'm stunned.
In your presence, I'm left paralyzed.
This feeling should be a crime.
I don't see how it's legalized.
You have me in overdrive.
I'm happier than a kid in a candy store.
I'm flying high, I'm going on tour.
I stop in my tracks when you walk through the
door.
The feeling in the pit of my stomach I think I
adore.
The love you give to me can't be disguised.
I see it when I look into your eyes.
The energy you give off gives me butterflies.

Author Bio

From the beginning, Monique Robinson beat the odds. She came into the world as a preemie. Monique knows what it means to be a warrior. Life sparked a fight in her early on. She was born in West Palm Beach and raised in the exquisite sunshine of Fort Pierce, Florida.

Monique began her writing journey in 2007. She was inspired to write after tragically losing her younger sister, *Darielle Robinson*. Monique used writing as her outlet to sustain herself in life. She was triumphant over many things that life had thrown at her. Monique's written poetic collection is diverse in both nature and style. Her poetry is sure to inspire, encourage, and transform lives alike.

Acknowledgments

I would like to thank God for blessing me with such a gift. I'm grateful he gave me the ability to put my thoughts on paper.

In memory of my father, ***Sammie Simmons***, thank you for all the lectures you gave to me. You never gave up on me. Thank you for believing in me when no one else did.

Raymond, I value you for being my listening ear when I needed it the most. You encouraged me to get back into writing. Raymond, you pushed me to continue despite obstacles that came my way.

Shaquinta Ingram, you brought all my creative ideas together. Thank you for making this book process so easy for me.

Lastly, thank you to all my family and friends. You all have supported me throughout this journey as well. It does not go unnoticed. So, from the bottom of my heart, I say thank you!